Exploring Moroccan Cuisine: 50 Recipes

By: Kelly Johnson

Table of Contents

- Chicken Tagine with Preserved Lemon and Olives
- Lamb Tagine with Prunes and Almonds
- Beef Tagine with Apricots
- Vegetable Tagine
- Seafood Tagine
- Kefta Tagine (Moroccan Meatball Tagine)
- Harira (Moroccan Lentil and Tomato Soup)
- Bissara (Fava Bean Soup)
- Moroccan Couscous with Seven Vegetables
- Lamb and Chickpea Couscous
- Seafood Couscous
- Chicken and Raisin Couscous
- Mechoui (Slow-Roasted Lamb)
- Rfissa (Chicken with Lentils and Msemen)
- Bastilla (Savory-Sweet Chicken Pie)
- Briouats (Savory Stuffed Pastries)
- Maakouda (Potato Fritters)
- Msemen (Layered Moroccan Pancakes)
- Baghrir (Moroccan Semolina Pancakes)
- Harcha (Semolina Flatbread)
- Beghrir (Honeycomb Pancakes)
- Khobz (Moroccan Round Bread)
- Batbout (Soft Moroccan Pita Bread)
- Zaalouk (Eggplant and Tomato Dip)
- Taktouka (Roasted Pepper and Tomato Salad)
- Moroccan Carrot Salad
- Orange and Olive Salad
- Moroccan Lentil Salad
- Moroccan Chickpea Salad
- Chermoula (Moroccan Marinade)
- Loubia (Moroccan White Bean Stew)
- Dchicha (Barley Soup)
- Sellou (Sweet Sesame and Almond Paste)
- Chebakia (Honey and Sesame Cookies)
- Ghriba (Almond and Coconut Cookies)

- Kaab el Ghazal (Gazelle Horn Pastries)
- Sfinge (Moroccan Doughnuts)
- Mhancha (Almond Snake Pastry)
- Fekkas (Moroccan Biscotti)
- Makroud (Date-Filled Semolina Cookies)
- Moroccan Mint Tea
- Amlou (Almond and Argan Oil Spread)
- Ras El Hanout (Moroccan Spice Blend)
- Stuffed Dates with Almond Paste
- Lamb with Honey and Almonds
- Moroccan Meatballs with Egg and Tomato Sauce
- Grilled Sardines with Chermoula
- Roasted Pepper and Eggplant Dip
- Moroccan Spiced Coffee
- Date and Almond Milkshake

Chicken Tagine with Preserved Lemon and Olives

Ingredients:

- 4 chicken thighs and drumsticks
- 1 preserved lemon, quartered
- 1 cup (150g) green olives
- 1 onion, chopped
- 3 cloves garlic, minced
- 1 teaspoon ground ginger
- 1 teaspoon turmeric
- 1 teaspoon paprika
- 1 teaspoon cumin
- ½ teaspoon cinnamon
- ¼ cup (60ml) olive oil
- 2 cups (480ml) chicken broth
- ¼ cup (15g) chopped cilantro

Instructions:

1. Heat oil in a tagine or pot, sauté onions and garlic.
2. Add chicken and brown on all sides.
3. Stir in spices and broth, cover, and simmer for 45 minutes.
4. Add preserved lemon and olives, cook for 10 more minutes.
5. Garnish with cilantro and serve with couscous.

Lamb Tagine with Prunes and Almonds

Ingredients:

- 2 lbs (900g) lamb shoulder, cubed
- 1 onion, chopped
- 3 cloves garlic, minced
- 1 teaspoon ground cinnamon
- 1 teaspoon ginger
- ½ teaspoon cumin
- ½ teaspoon salt
- 2 tablespoons honey
- 1 cup (150g) prunes
- ½ cup (60g) almonds, toasted
- ¼ cup (15g) chopped cilantro
- 2 cups (480ml) beef broth

Instructions:

1. Brown lamb in a tagine or pot with oil.
2. Add onion, garlic, and spices, sauté for 5 minutes.
3. Pour in broth and simmer for 1 ½ hours.
4. Stir in prunes and honey, cook for another 20 minutes.
5. Garnish with almonds and cilantro.

Beef Tagine with Apricots

Ingredients:

- 2 lbs (900g) beef chuck, cubed
- 1 onion, chopped
- 3 cloves garlic, minced
- 1 teaspoon cinnamon
- 1 teaspoon paprika
- 1 teaspoon ginger
- ½ teaspoon salt
- 1 cup (150g) dried apricots
- 2 tablespoons honey
- 2 cups (480ml) beef broth

Instructions:

1. Sauté beef, onion, and garlic in oil.
2. Add spices and broth, simmer for 1 ½ hours.
3. Add apricots and honey, cook for 20 more minutes.
4. Serve with couscous or bread.

Vegetable Tagine

Ingredients:

- 2 carrots, sliced
- 1 zucchini, sliced
- 1 eggplant, chopped
- 1 bell pepper, sliced
- 1 onion, chopped
- 3 cloves garlic, minced
- 1 teaspoon paprika
- 1 teaspoon cumin
- ½ teaspoon cinnamon
- 1 can (15 oz) chickpeas, drained
- 2 cups (480ml) vegetable broth

Instructions:

1. Heat oil in a tagine, sauté onion and garlic.
2. Add vegetables, chickpeas, spices, and broth.
3. Simmer for 40 minutes until tender.

Seafood Tagine

Ingredients:

- 1 lb (450g) white fish (cod, halibut), cut into chunks
- ½ lb (225g) shrimp, peeled
- 1 onion, chopped
- 2 tomatoes, chopped
- 3 cloves garlic, minced
- 1 teaspoon paprika
- 1 teaspoon cumin
- ½ teaspoon salt
- ¼ teaspoon saffron
- 2 tablespoons olive oil
- ½ cup (120ml) fish stock

Instructions:

1. Sauté onion, garlic, and tomatoes in oil.
2. Add spices and fish stock.
3. Add fish and shrimp, simmer for 15 minutes.

Kefta Tagine (Moroccan Meatball Tagine)

Ingredients:

- 1 lb (450g) ground beef or lamb
- 1 teaspoon cumin
- 1 teaspoon paprika
- ½ teaspoon cinnamon
- ½ teaspoon salt
- 2 tablespoons chopped parsley
- 1 onion, chopped
- 3 cloves garlic, minced
- 1 cup (240ml) tomato sauce

Instructions:

1. Mix beef with spices and parsley, shape into meatballs.
2. Sauté onion and garlic, add tomato sauce and simmer for 10 minutes.
3. Add meatballs and cook for 20 minutes.

Harira (Moroccan Lentil and Tomato Soup)

Ingredients:

- 1 cup (200g) lentils
- ½ cup (100g) chickpeas, soaked overnight
- 1 onion, chopped
- 2 tomatoes, blended
- 3 cloves garlic, minced
- 1 teaspoon cumin
- 1 teaspoon paprika
- ½ teaspoon cinnamon
- 6 cups (1.5L) vegetable broth

Instructions:

1. Sauté onion, garlic, and spices.
2. Add tomatoes, broth, lentils, and chickpeas. Simmer for 1 hour.

Bissara (Fava Bean Soup)

Ingredients:

- 2 cups (400g) dried fava beans, soaked overnight
- 3 cloves garlic, minced
- 1 teaspoon cumin
- ½ teaspoon salt
- 4 cups (1L) water
- ¼ cup (60ml) olive oil

Instructions:

1. Boil fava beans with garlic and salt for 40 minutes.
2. Blend until smooth, drizzle with olive oil.

Moroccan Couscous with Seven Vegetables

Ingredients:

- 2 cups (400g) couscous
- 2 carrots, sliced
- 1 zucchini, sliced
- 1 eggplant, chopped
- 1 turnip, diced
- 1 onion, chopped
- 1 can (15 oz) chickpeas, drained
- 1 teaspoon cumin
- 1 teaspoon paprika
- 4 cups (1L) vegetable broth

Instructions:

1. Sauté onion and vegetables in oil.
2. Add chickpeas, spices, and broth, simmer for 30 minutes.
3. Steam couscous and serve with vegetables.

Lamb and Chickpea Couscous

Ingredients:

- 2 lbs (900g) lamb, cubed
- 1 cup (200g) chickpeas, soaked overnight
- 1 onion, chopped
- 2 carrots, sliced
- 2 zucchini, sliced
- 1 teaspoon cumin
- 1 teaspoon paprika
- 4 cups (1L) broth

Instructions:

1. Brown lamb, add onion, carrots, and spices.
2. Add chickpeas and broth, simmer for 1 ½ hours.
3. Serve over couscous.

Seafood Couscous

Ingredients:

- 1 lb (450g) white fish, cut into chunks
- ½ lb (225g) shrimp, peeled
- 1 onion, chopped
- 2 tomatoes, chopped
- 3 cloves garlic, minced
- 1 teaspoon paprika
- 1 teaspoon cumin
- ½ teaspoon salt
- 2 cups (400g) couscous
- 4 cups (1L) fish broth

Instructions:

1. Sauté onion, garlic, and tomatoes. Add spices and fish broth.
2. Add fish and shrimp, cook for 10 minutes.
3. Serve over couscous.

Chicken and Raisin Couscous

Ingredients:

- 2 cups (400g) couscous
- 2 lbs (900g) chicken thighs
- 1 onion, chopped
- 2 cloves garlic, minced
- 1 teaspoon ground ginger
- 1 teaspoon cinnamon
- ½ teaspoon turmeric
- ½ teaspoon cumin
- ½ cup (75g) raisins
- ¼ cup (60ml) honey
- 3 cups (720ml) chicken broth
- ¼ cup (15g) chopped almonds

Instructions:

1. Sauté onion and garlic in a pot. Add chicken and brown on all sides.
2. Stir in spices, broth, raisins, and honey. Simmer for 45 minutes.
3. Steam couscous and serve with chicken, garnished with almonds.

Mechoui (Slow-Roasted Lamb)

Ingredients:

- 1 whole leg of lamb (about 5 lbs)
- 2 tablespoons butter, melted
- 2 tablespoons olive oil
- 1 teaspoon cumin
- 1 teaspoon paprika
- 1 teaspoon salt
- ½ teaspoon black pepper
- 4 cloves garlic, minced

Instructions:

1. Preheat oven to 325°F (165°C).
2. Mix butter, oil, and spices, rub all over lamb.
3. Place in a roasting pan and cover with foil.
4. Roast for 4-5 hours, basting occasionally.

Rfissa (Chicken with Lentils and Msemen)

Ingredients:

- 1 whole chicken, cut into pieces
- 1 onion, chopped
- 2 cloves garlic, minced
- 1 teaspoon ground ginger
- 1 teaspoon turmeric
- ½ teaspoon cinnamon
- ½ teaspoon black pepper
- 1 cup (200g) lentils
- 4 cups (1L) chicken broth
- 4 Msemen (see recipe below)

Instructions:

1. Sauté onion, garlic, and spices in a pot. Add chicken and brown on all sides.
2. Add lentils and broth, simmer for 1 hour.
3. Serve over torn pieces of Msemen.

Bastilla (Savory-Sweet Chicken Pie)

Ingredients:

- 2 lbs (900g) chicken thighs
- 1 onion, chopped
- 3 cloves garlic, minced
- 1 teaspoon cinnamon
- 1 teaspoon ground ginger
- ½ teaspoon turmeric
- ½ teaspoon salt
- 3 eggs, beaten
- ½ cup (75g) almonds, toasted and chopped
- ½ cup (75g) powdered sugar
- 8 sheets phyllo dough
- ½ cup (120g) butter, melted

Instructions:

1. Sauté onion, garlic, and spices in a pot. Add chicken and cook until tender.
2. Shred chicken, mix with beaten eggs, almonds, and sugar.
3. Layer phyllo dough in a baking dish, add filling, and top with more phyllo.
4. Brush with butter and bake at 375°F (190°C) for 30 minutes.

Briouats (Savory Stuffed Pastries)

Ingredients:

- 1 lb (450g) ground beef or chicken
- 1 onion, chopped
- 2 cloves garlic, minced
- 1 teaspoon ground ginger
- ½ teaspoon cumin
- ½ teaspoon salt
- 8 sheets phyllo dough
- ½ cup (120g) butter, melted

Instructions:

1. Sauté onion, garlic, and meat with spices. Let cool.
2. Cut phyllo sheets into strips, add filling, and fold into triangles.
3. Brush with butter and bake at 375°F (190°C) for 20 minutes.

Maakouda (Potato Fritters)

Ingredients:

- 3 potatoes, boiled and mashed
- 1 egg
- ½ cup (60g) flour
- 1 teaspoon cumin
- ½ teaspoon salt
- ½ teaspoon paprika
- Oil for frying

Instructions:

1. Mix mashed potatoes with egg, flour, and spices.
2. Shape into patties and fry in oil until golden.

Msemen (Layered Moroccan Pancakes)

Ingredients:

- 2 cups (250g) all-purpose flour
- 1 cup (125g) semolina
- 1 teaspoon salt
- 1 teaspoon sugar
- ¾ cup (180ml) warm water
- ¼ cup (60ml) melted butter

Instructions:

1. Mix flour, semolina, salt, and sugar, then knead with water. Let rest for 30 minutes.
2. Divide dough, roll out thin, brush with butter, and fold into squares.
3. Cook on a griddle for 2 minutes per side.

Baghrir (Moroccan Semolina Pancakes)

Ingredients:

- 2 cups (250g) semolina
- 1 cup (125g) all-purpose flour
- 1 teaspoon yeast
- ½ teaspoon salt
- 2 ½ cups (600ml) warm water

Instructions:

1. Blend all ingredients and let rest for 1 hour.
2. Cook on a non-stick pan without flipping.

Harcha (Semolina Flatbread)

Ingredients:

- 2 cups (250g) fine semolina
- 1 teaspoon baking powder
- ½ teaspoon salt
- ¼ cup (60ml) melted butter
- ½ cup (120ml) milk

Instructions:

1. Mix semolina, baking powder, and salt. Stir in butter and milk.
2. Shape into discs and cook on a griddle for 3 minutes per side.

Beghrir (Honeycomb Pancakes)

Ingredients:

- 2 cups (250g) semolina
- 1 cup (125g) all-purpose flour
- 1 teaspoon yeast
- ½ teaspoon salt
- 2 ½ cups (600ml) warm water

Instructions:

1. Blend all ingredients and let rest for 1 hour.
2. Cook on a non-stick pan without flipping until bubbles form.

Khobz (Moroccan Round Bread)

Ingredients:

- 4 cups (500g) all-purpose flour
- 1 tablespoon sugar
- 2 teaspoons salt
- 2 teaspoons yeast
- 1 ½ cups (360ml) warm water
- 2 tablespoons olive oil

Instructions:

1. Mix flour, sugar, salt, and yeast. Add water and oil, knead for 10 minutes.
2. Let rise for 1 hour, then divide into two balls and flatten into rounds.
3. Let rise for 30 more minutes.
4. Bake at 375°F (190°C) for 25 minutes until golden.

Batbout (Soft Moroccan Pita Bread)

Ingredients:

- 3 cups (375g) all-purpose flour
- 1 cup (125g) fine semolina
- 2 teaspoons yeast
- 1 teaspoon salt
- 1 ½ cups (360ml) warm water

Instructions:

1. Mix flour, semolina, yeast, and salt. Add water and knead for 10 minutes.
2. Let rise for 1 hour, then divide into small balls and flatten into discs.
3. Let rise for 30 minutes.
4. Cook on a dry pan for 2 minutes per side until puffed and golden.

Zaalouk (Eggplant and Tomato Dip)

Ingredients:

- 2 eggplants, diced
- 3 tomatoes, chopped
- 3 cloves garlic, minced
- 1 teaspoon paprika
- 1 teaspoon cumin
- ½ teaspoon salt
- 2 tablespoons olive oil
- ¼ cup (15g) chopped cilantro

Instructions:

1. Boil eggplants until soft, then drain and mash.
2. Sauté garlic and tomatoes in olive oil.
3. Add mashed eggplant, spices, and cilantro. Simmer for 10 minutes.

Taktouka (Roasted Pepper and Tomato Salad)

Ingredients:

- 2 roasted bell peppers, chopped
- 3 tomatoes, chopped
- 2 cloves garlic, minced
- 1 teaspoon paprika
- 1 teaspoon cumin
- ½ teaspoon salt
- 2 tablespoons olive oil

Instructions:

1. Sauté garlic and tomatoes in olive oil until soft.
2. Add roasted bell peppers and spices. Simmer for 10 minutes.

Moroccan Carrot Salad

Ingredients:

- 4 carrots, sliced
- 2 tablespoons olive oil
- 1 teaspoon cumin
- 1 teaspoon paprika
- ½ teaspoon salt
- 1 tablespoon lemon juice
- ¼ cup (15g) chopped parsley

Instructions:

1. Boil carrots until tender, then drain.
2. Toss with olive oil, spices, lemon juice, and parsley.

Orange and Olive Salad

Ingredients:

- 2 oranges, peeled and sliced
- ½ cup (75g) black olives
- 1 tablespoon olive oil
- ½ teaspoon cinnamon
- ¼ teaspoon salt
- ¼ cup (15g) chopped mint

Instructions:

1. Arrange orange slices on a plate.
2. Top with olives, drizzle with olive oil, and sprinkle with cinnamon and salt.
3. Garnish with mint.

Moroccan Lentil Salad

Ingredients:

- 1 cup (200g) lentils, cooked
- 1 small onion, chopped
- 1 small tomato, chopped
- ¼ cup (15g) chopped cilantro
- 2 tablespoons olive oil
- 1 teaspoon cumin
- ½ teaspoon salt
- 1 tablespoon lemon juice

Instructions:

1. Mix lentils, onion, tomato, and cilantro.
2. Toss with olive oil, cumin, salt, and lemon juice.

Moroccan Chickpea Salad

Ingredients:

- 1 can (15 oz) chickpeas, drained
- 1 small cucumber, diced
- 1 small red onion, chopped
- 1 small tomato, diced
- ¼ cup (15g) chopped parsley
- 2 tablespoons olive oil
- 1 teaspoon cumin
- ½ teaspoon salt
- 1 tablespoon lemon juice

Instructions:

1. Mix chickpeas, cucumber, onion, tomato, and parsley.
2. Toss with olive oil, cumin, salt, and lemon juice.

Chermoula (Moroccan Marinade)

Ingredients:

- ½ cup (15g) chopped parsley
- ½ cup (15g) chopped cilantro
- 2 cloves garlic, minced
- 1 teaspoon paprika
- 1 teaspoon cumin
- ½ teaspoon salt
- ¼ teaspoon cayenne pepper
- ¼ cup (60ml) olive oil
- 1 tablespoon lemon juice

Instructions:

1. Mix all ingredients in a bowl.
2. Use as a marinade for fish, chicken, or vegetables.

Loubia (Moroccan White Bean Stew)

Ingredients:

- 2 cups (400g) white beans, soaked overnight
- 1 small onion, chopped
- 3 cloves garlic, minced
- 2 tomatoes, chopped
- 1 teaspoon paprika
- 1 teaspoon cumin
- ½ teaspoon salt
- 2 tablespoons olive oil
- 4 cups (1L) water

Instructions:

1. Sauté onion, garlic, and tomatoes in olive oil.
2. Add beans, spices, and water.
3. Simmer for 1 hour until beans are tender.

Dchicha (Barley Soup)

Ingredients:

- 1 cup (200g) barley grits
- 1 small onion, chopped
- 2 cloves garlic, minced
- 1 teaspoon cumin
- ½ teaspoon paprika
- ½ teaspoon salt
- 1 tablespoon olive oil
- 5 cups (1.2L) water
- ¼ cup (15g) chopped cilantro

Instructions:

1. Heat olive oil in a pot and sauté onion and garlic.
2. Add barley grits, spices, and water. Simmer for 30 minutes.
3. Stir in cilantro before serving.

Sellou (Sweet Sesame and Almond Paste)

Ingredients:

- 2 cups (250g) flour
- 1 cup (150g) almonds, toasted and ground
- 1 cup (150g) sesame seeds, toasted and ground
- 1 teaspoon cinnamon
- ½ teaspoon anise powder
- ½ teaspoon salt
- 1 cup (200g) powdered sugar
- ½ cup (120ml) melted butter
- ½ cup (120ml) honey

Instructions:

1. Toast flour in a dry pan until golden.
2. Mix with almonds, sesame, cinnamon, anise, salt, and sugar.
3. Stir in melted butter and honey until a paste forms.
4. Press into a dish or roll into balls.

Chebakia (Honey and Sesame Cookies)

Ingredients:

- 2 cups (250g) flour
- 1 teaspoon cinnamon
- ½ teaspoon anise powder
- ½ teaspoon salt
- 1 tablespoon orange blossom water
- ½ cup (120ml) melted butter
- 1 egg
- ½ cup (75g) toasted sesame seeds
- 1 cup (250ml) honey
- Oil for frying

Instructions:

1. Mix flour, cinnamon, anise, salt, orange blossom water, butter, and egg into a dough. Let rest for 30 minutes.
2. Roll out dough and cut into strips, twisting into flower shapes.
3. Fry in hot oil until golden, then dip in warm honey.
4. Sprinkle with sesame seeds.

Ghriba (Almond and Coconut Cookies)

Ingredients:

- 1 cup (100g) almond flour
- 1 cup (100g) shredded coconut
- ½ cup (100g) sugar
- 1 teaspoon baking powder
- 2 eggs
- ½ teaspoon orange blossom water

Instructions:

1. Mix all ingredients into a dough.
2. Shape into small balls and flatten slightly.
3. Bake at 350°F (175°C) for 15 minutes.

Kaab el Ghazal (Gazelle Horn Pastries)

Ingredients:

For the filling:

- 2 cups (250g) almond flour
- ½ cup (100g) powdered sugar
- ½ teaspoon cinnamon
- 2 tablespoons orange blossom water

For the dough:

- 2 cups (250g) all-purpose flour
- ½ teaspoon salt
- ¼ cup (60ml) melted butter
- ½ cup (120ml) water

Instructions:

1. Mix filling ingredients into a paste.
2. Mix dough ingredients and roll out thin.
3. Fill with almond paste, shape into crescents, and seal.
4. Bake at 350°F (175°C) for 20 minutes.

Sfinge (Moroccan Doughnuts)

Ingredients:

- 2 cups (250g) all-purpose flour
- 1 teaspoon yeast
- ½ teaspoon salt
- ¾ cup (180ml) warm water
- Oil for frying
- Sugar for dusting

Instructions:

1. Mix flour, yeast, salt, and water into a sticky dough. Let rise for 1 hour.
2. Shape into rings and fry until golden.
3. Dust with sugar before serving.

Mhancha (Almond Snake Pastry)

Ingredients:

- 2 cups (250g) almond flour
- ½ cup (100g) powdered sugar
- ½ teaspoon cinnamon
- 2 tablespoons orange blossom water
- 8 sheets phyllo dough
- ½ cup (120g) melted butter
- ½ cup (120ml) honey

Instructions:

1. Mix almond flour, sugar, cinnamon, and orange blossom water into a paste.
2. Roll into a long rope and wrap in phyllo dough, forming a spiral shape.
3. Brush with butter and bake at 375°F (190°C) for 20 minutes.
4. Drizzle with honey before serving.

Fekkas (Moroccan Biscotti)

Ingredients:

- 2 cups (250g) all-purpose flour
- ½ cup (100g) sugar
- 1 teaspoon baking powder
- ½ teaspoon salt
- ½ teaspoon anise seeds
- ½ cup (75g) almonds, chopped
- 2 eggs
- ¼ cup (60ml) vegetable oil

Instructions:

1. Mix flour, sugar, baking powder, salt, anise, and almonds.
2. Add eggs and oil, knead into a dough.
3. Shape into logs and bake at 350°F (175°C) for 20 minutes.
4. Slice and bake again for 10 minutes until crisp.

Makroud (Date-Filled Semolina Cookies)

Ingredients:

For the dough:

- 2 cups (250g) semolina
- ½ teaspoon salt
- ½ cup (120ml) melted butter
- ½ cup (120ml) water

For the filling:

- 1 cup (200g) dates, mashed
- ½ teaspoon cinnamon
- 1 tablespoon orange blossom water

Instructions:

1. Mix dough ingredients and knead lightly.
2. Mix filling ingredients into a paste.
3. Roll out dough, place filling in the center, and fold over.
4. Cut into diamond shapes and fry until golden.

Moroccan Mint Tea

Ingredients:

- 4 cups (1L) boiling water
- 2 tablespoons green tea leaves
- 1 bunch fresh mint
- ¼ cup (50g) sugar

Instructions:

1. Brew green tea leaves in boiling water for 5 minutes.
2. Add mint and sugar, steep for another 5 minutes.
3. Pour from high to create foam before serving.

Amlou (Almond and Argan Oil Spread)

Ingredients:

- 1 cup (150g) almonds, toasted and ground
- ¼ cup (60ml) argan oil
- ¼ cup (60ml) honey

Instructions:

1. Blend almonds, argan oil, and honey into a smooth paste.
2. Serve with bread or pastries.

Ras El Hanout (Moroccan Spice Blend)

Ingredients:

- 1 teaspoon ground cumin
- 1 teaspoon ground coriander
- 1 teaspoon ground ginger
- 1 teaspoon paprika
- 1 teaspoon turmeric
- ½ teaspoon ground cinnamon
- ½ teaspoon ground black pepper
- ½ teaspoon ground cardamom
- ½ teaspoon ground nutmeg
- ¼ teaspoon cayenne pepper
- ¼ teaspoon ground cloves

Instructions:

1. Mix all spices together and store in an airtight container.
2. Use in Moroccan stews, meats, and vegetable dishes.

Stuffed Dates with Almond Paste

Ingredients:

- 12 Medjool dates, pitted
- ½ cup (75g) blanched almonds
- 1 tablespoon powdered sugar
- ½ teaspoon cinnamon
- 1 teaspoon orange blossom water

Instructions:

1. Blend almonds, sugar, cinnamon, and orange blossom water into a paste.
2. Stuff each date with a small amount of almond paste.

Lamb with Honey and Almonds

Ingredients:

- 2 lbs (900g) lamb shoulder, cubed
- 1 onion, chopped
- 3 cloves garlic, minced
- 1 teaspoon Ras El Hanout
- 1 teaspoon cinnamon
- ½ teaspoon salt
- ¼ cup (60ml) honey
- ½ cup (75g) almonds, toasted
- 2 cups (480ml) beef broth

Instructions:

1. Brown lamb in a tagine or pot.
2. Add onion, garlic, and spices, and sauté for 5 minutes.
3. Pour in broth, cover, and simmer for 1 ½ hours.
4. Stir in honey and almonds, cook for another 10 minutes.

Moroccan Meatballs with Egg and Tomato Sauce

Ingredients:

For the meatballs:

- 1 lb (450g) ground beef or lamb
- 1 teaspoon cumin
- 1 teaspoon paprika
- ½ teaspoon cinnamon
- ½ teaspoon salt
- ¼ cup (15g) chopped parsley

For the sauce:

- 1 onion, chopped
- 3 cloves garlic, minced
- 2 cups (480ml) tomato sauce
- 1 teaspoon Ras El Hanout
- 4 eggs

Instructions:

1. Mix meatball ingredients, shape into small balls, and brown in a pan.
2. Sauté onion and garlic, add tomato sauce and spices.
3. Add meatballs, cover, and simmer for 20 minutes.
4. Crack eggs into the sauce and cook until set.

Grilled Sardines with Chermoula

Ingredients:

- 1 lb (450g) fresh sardines, cleaned
- ½ cup (15g) chopped parsley
- ½ cup (15g) chopped cilantro
- 2 cloves garlic, minced
- 1 teaspoon cumin
- 1 teaspoon paprika
- ½ teaspoon salt
- ¼ cup (60ml) olive oil
- 2 tablespoons lemon juice

Instructions:

1. Mix chermoula marinade ingredients.
2. Coat sardines with the marinade and let sit for 30 minutes.
3. Grill for 3-4 minutes per side.

Roasted Pepper and Eggplant Dip

Ingredients:

- 2 roasted bell peppers, chopped
- 1 small eggplant, roasted and mashed
- 2 cloves garlic, minced
- 1 teaspoon cumin
- 1 teaspoon paprika
- ½ teaspoon salt
- 2 tablespoons olive oil

Instructions:

1. Sauté garlic in olive oil.
2. Add roasted peppers, mashed eggplant, and spices.
3. Cook for 10 minutes and serve with bread.

Moroccan Spiced Coffee

Ingredients:

- 2 cups (480ml) strong brewed coffee
- ½ teaspoon cinnamon
- ¼ teaspoon ground cardamom
- ¼ teaspoon ground nutmeg
- ¼ teaspoon ground cloves
- 1 tablespoon sugar (optional)

Instructions:

1. Brew coffee and stir in spices.
2. Sweeten with sugar if desired.

Date and Almond Milkshake

Ingredients:

- 1 cup (240ml) almond milk
- 6 Medjool dates, pitted
- ¼ teaspoon cinnamon
- ½ teaspoon vanilla extract
- ½ cup (120ml) ice

Instructions:

1. Blend all ingredients until smooth.